POEMS
for
PALESTINE

POEMS
for
PALESTINE

Edited by Maher J. Massis, Ph.D.

Published by Hesperus Press Limited
28 Mortimer Street, London W1W 7RD
www.hesperuspress.com

Poems for Palestine first published by Hesperus Press Limited, 2015
Poems for Palestine © 2015 Maher Massis

Designed and typeset by Roland Codd
Printed in Great Britain by CPI Group (UK) Ltd, CR0 4YY

ISBN: 978-1-84391-551-5

For the People of Palestine
and their supporters
throughout the world

CONTENTS

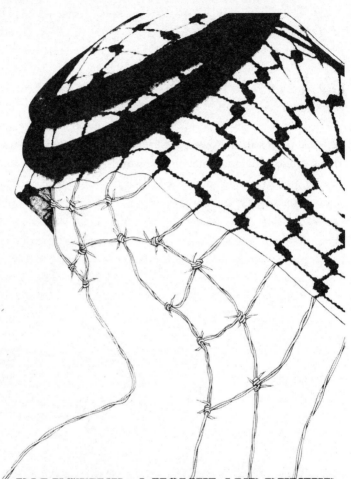

PALESTINE : A HOMELAND DENIED

INTRODUCTION

Over the years I have come across many poems written about Palestine – some from magazines, and others from forwarded emails, blogs, Facebook posts etc. I was truly impressed by many of these poems that showed the untapped talent that was out there. These individuals may not be world-renowned poets but instead are just people going about their daily lives who once in a while become inspired to write a poem. I found myself actively seeking out these poems and realised how difficult it was to find them since they were scattered everywhere. So I embarked on a project to create a forum, through the cyber space medium of www.poems4palestine.com to which anyone can upload a poem for the world to see and enjoy.

The next step of the project was to publish an anthology of selected poems from the website. This anthology is not only a work of literary art but also a fundraising exercise since the proceeds from the sale of these books will be donated to a US registered non-profit organization, Palestine Children's Relief Fund (www.pcrf.net). Since 1991, PCRF has provided desperately needed medical relief to Palestinian children and other Arab children. From cancer treatment to treating children with severe burns resulting from Israel's use of phosphorous bombs, the organisation has been relentless in its hard work and dedication.

This book is the first publication and the hope is for the website to continue to attract more poems for future volumes.

'Um Fillistina'

by Amanda Dhaber

Um Fillistina
Olive groves like an undulating jade sea
Orchards of oranges unnamed
Stone latticework like white picket fences
Fellah homes in suburban bliss
Starling and lark – nest, breed, sing
Baladi, Baladi
Expulsion… Eviction… Red-lined Map…
Olive groves like a maelstrom
Fierce waves of shamouti crash
Stone walls leveled
Mud hut wasteland
Starling and lark, homeless, barren, lament
Baladi, Baladi
Um Hazeena

'I Am'

by Arwa Abou El Hassan

I am the voice of the girl who cried out loud
When her mom got shot in the Palestine crowd

I am the tears of the Father who got thrown in jail
Because his country was taken by Israel

I am the blood that's dripping from the innocent's wounds
When they tried to defend themselves but are now forever
 doomed.

I am the stone being held in the little boy's hand
For all he wants to do is to defend his precious land

I am the scream that came out from a mother as she saw
Her little young ones being taken away without any law

I am the innocent standing in front of the tank
The same one you paid for with the taxes from your bank

I am the soul that's wandering around in the dead's fields
Cause they all went away... they didn't have any shields
I'm the home being torn apart but no one's listening...
Cause you don't care about those they're imprisoning

I am the country striving to keep my home
While Americans worry about their Google Chrome

I am the girl standing here, but all I can do
Is rhyme this poem and point at you...

I am the hope sitting in everyone's hearts,
Cause we need to free Palestine, yes we got to start

I am freedom coming to you in the nearest time
Only when you learn to give up your dime

I am Palestine, yes you've now read it all
Will you help me... or just leave me to fall?

Journey into a New Life

by Jamal Krayem Kanj

Leaving was so sudden
The Camp was harsh abode
Yet, it was my heaven
Leaving the Camp was forebode
For migration was focused driven
Rooted in life of despair
Entrant for migration and transfer
On the deck, I waved goodbye
To the dark dock, one last time
Quivering lips and soggy eyes
As the ship sailed in the dark sky
A young man stands alone petrify.
Raised for transplantation
But unlike a deep rooted tree
Transferred absent of foliation.
My uprooting meant to set me free
Of course, the tree will likely endure
But her longing has no cure
The tree may survive
But to the fullest it will not thrive
The tree may mature strong
But in the new home, it will not belong
The ship sailed into the deep sea
While my heart wasn't moving along
A single moon and a star
Sharing my darkest night
Looking to the Camp from afar

Remembering those I left in the plight
Forward looking, I saw a streak of light
From the sea, the sun started to rise
The new shores were strikingly bright
Another day, another land, I started to realize
I managed to smile, with sadness in my eyes
For exodus is the Camp's denizens' prize
But it must be recorded, it has to be written
Those I left behind, will never be forgotten
Despite the hard life, the Camp remains my heaven

A Journey to See Where I Was to Be

by Fadi Zanayed

I was just below the cloud
The sound of thunder was ever so loud
My wings were spread I was actually flying
My speed was way past soaring
A white dove was leading my way
We will be there in less than a day
I was excited yet not joyfully
I embarked on my mission painfully
The dove wanted me to see
Where I was to be
But through her intervention
I was routed in a different direction
She told me she was my greatest option
Yet not my only solution
She urged me not to employ the other
For it would lead to the death of me and my brother
Nearing the end of our trip
I was perplexed about what came from her lip
When she said, I cannot go any further
Don't tell anyone not even a murmur
But why I stopped and questioned
Waiting a while before I was answered
Finally she said, I cannot bear to see what you will see
For a black hawk is what I will be
And I replied, What about the other solution
How can I see and still choose you as my option
She answered, You will need the threat of the other solution

To maintain me as your option
She then gave me directions and off I went
To the place I was to be sent
It was not hard to find
For it has been forever a picture inside my mind
I went in for the approach
Not knowing upon what I will encroach
I was greeted with great hospitality
Overwhelmed at the degree of their generosity
I saw their misery, I saw their pain
What do they do about the rain?
Suddenly it rained from above
And I knew it was a signal from the dove
I asked for water to drink
It had to be fetched for there was no sink
When they eat and dine
They always finish the meal with a discussion on Palestine
I wondered as I looked to the sky
Why can't God hear the cry
For the return to our country
And the restoration of our dignity
Near the end of another sleepless night
I awoke to a faint light
It was still dark in the camp
For there is no street lamp
I walked through and through
Not knowing what to do
About the guilt within me
And about the horror that I see
Then I wondered what if I were here
And another was there

What would I want him to do
As he is living his life through
And suddenly my image appeared
It was a scene I feared
I looked around for the others
What was the fate of my parents and brothers
I saw my mother sitting all alone
Where was my father, was he gone
I walked through the door
Where was my older brother, was he at war?
I knelt to the ground and wept
Hitting the dirt with a big welt
I cried out with a loud voice
There is only one option one choice
And there I was flying again
Was this part of the dove's plan
My flight soon approached the sea
As the dove reappeared in front of me
She was silent most of the way
Not wondering about what I had to say
My wings were stretched ever so wide
Like the wings of a black hawk from side to side
She looked back and said with a smile
Ahead of us is many a mile
You still have either option
But only one solution

As Palestine Cries

by Shomaila Shakur

As Palestine cries,
children weep
parents cry
sisters get raped
and brothers die.

As Palestine cries,
people see their land in ruins
the crops have died
innocent people pass away
all their life they tried.

As Palestine cries
the bloodstream gets bigger
innocent youths are forced to pull the trigger
their feelings represented by lightning and thunder
most of the people are six feet under.

As Palestine cries
the ground begins to crack
it weeps tears of blood,
so many people dead,
more than a thousand youths not fed.

As Palestine cries,
children weep
parents cry
sisters get raped
and brothers die.

Palestine did cry
Palestine is crying
and as Palestine cries,
every ounce of blood
shed by the Palestinians for their land
will not go to waste
they will be united, and one day –
Palestine
will stand.

Quick Thinking

by L. Al-Ahmad

Bitter.
Like a glass of occupation.
No flavour.
Just the taste of oppression.
No colour.
Just the shadows of isolation.
A world filled with empty promises. Like the bankruptcy of
    justice.
No truth – just lies on credit.
Instead of giving us a solution and leaving us to spread it,
they give us plastic and tell us to spend it
And how far does it take us when each swipe buys injustice?
When each dollar is encrusted with a politician's corruption?

They say normalize and move on and worry only about
    tomorrow.
That the world is doing just fine, so don't overthink or be too
    thorough
when seeking the truth you know only as you are told,
so the truth does not hold and you accept the status quo
because they say
that it is so.

But your brain has been wiped out like a bank account hit by
    Madoff.
And that's the tradeoff when you sell out for a quick payoff.
Perhaps it's time to cash the reality check you've neglected
and try to get connected with the truth that you've rejected.
Then our resistance will be resurrected and our efforts can be
    redirected
to those who are affected rather than to our days filled with
    emptiness
and we can redeem for our lack of purpose
and rid the bitterness in this ale of
prejudice.

Life in Palestine

by Shomaila Shakur

It's six am in the morning, I've only just seen this world.
The fresh scent of thisland –
My land,
Which I've been brought into.
My mother clings on to me,
As it sounds like a stampede going past
'Mum look! Dad's playing with a soldier' –
They take him down with a blast.
My mother weeps and explains to me
my father's gone
He's FREE.
As years go past, at least three or four,
I wonder about
my Land, I want to know more.
As I grew older I'd ask my mum
'when will we be
FREE?'
I look around to see
my land,
There's nothing left, I wonder why people
unknown to me
have given money to plant these trees.
I stood like a soldier
as I feel a sudden force coming my way
'MUM!'
that's the only word I had a chance to say.
I'm dominated by darkness, I can't see a thing

but then I open my eyes and hear them sing
I'm not alone in this place there's people of my own kind
I can see my dad running to me – his words
'You're in a better place
You're FREE'
I view the world below me
only to see my people die.
'I'm in a better place now mum
but I promise I did try.'
We all close our eyes to open them and see
we've washed away today's
bloodstream.
The angels start singing, I look behind me,
'It's been a long time, but I'm glad
you're FREE.'

Gazan War Child

by Sondos Alqadri

I am a Palestinian child. I live in Gaza
But that is not really my full definition
It doesn't say much
So let me start again and explain my dilemma
I am a Palestinian war child living in occupied Gaza
Yep, much better. But it's still missing some detail
I am a paralyzed, Palestinian war child living in occupied,
    besieged Gaza
That doesn't cover a simple part of the matter!
I am a paralyzed, disfigured, Palestinian war child living in
    occupied, besieged, oppressed Gaza
Oh dear, my vocabulary has become too weak. I haven't been
    to school ever since it happened
If I only had a dictionary, I see all the other kids carrying one.
They say it has all the words you can think of! At least that's
    what my neighbor told me
You probably know my neighbor. He's the clean, dressy, smart
    kid every mother would fall in love with.
He passes by me every morning with a friendly grin on his face
He lent me his dictionary once to look into
Oh, was I impressed by the number of words in that thick
    book
I got so excited flipping page after the other
He looked down on me with both compassion and surprise
He asked, 'Haven't you ever seen a dictionary before?'
My face reddened with shame, and replied with a soft voice,
    'No, I haven't'

He smiled at me with that sweet pleasant face I was used to
    seeing every morning
Then he added, 'Would you like to keep it?'
My eyes widened, and my face glowed with delight
'I'd Love to! Can you help me look for the word "Palestinian"
    in it?'
I could tell from his features that he was shocked by my request
He answered, 'Waseem, I don't believe they have that word in
    the dictionary.'
Now it was my turn for shock to take over my features
'But… But... You mean there is no "Palestinian" in there?'
Somehow, my impression towards that book I had gone
    through savagely seconds ago
 turned into disgust...
I threw it away. I couldn't bear the level of denial directed to
    me from a silly book
Between the folds of that massive book, I couldn't find the
    word that describes me best
Therefore, I will use my own words to tell my tragic story...

I am a Palestinian war child
In case you don't know what 'Palestinian' means
It means when they write about us in newspapers
All you do is toss them in your trash piled

It's when every kid in the world has his protected rights
While you are left out neglected, on the sidelines unrecognized
It's when children like me get cruelly killed
And the world still can't tell whether we're terrorists or
    terrorized

I am a Palestinian war child, and I live in Gaza
Do you know what 'Gaza' means?
It means a place where heroes like me come from
It means kids like me becoming grown-ups by the age of seven,
becoming men by ten, and warriors by eleven

I am a Gazan War Child
Are you aware of the word 'CHILD'
I look at other children in different parts of the world
They hold crayons and coloring books while I hold a sword
They'd be learning to count on these colorful counters
While I am playing with my own life counter

I am a Gazan war child
Do you know the meaning of war?
It means the loss of family members, the loss of friends
It means amputating one of your limbs or both, it depends
It means deformation by raining acid and phosphorus bombs
It means watching people getting butchered in the middle of
    the pogrom
It means torn down houses, mosques and schools
It means having to surrender to the Jungle rules
It means me seeing the world in black and white
Like history repeating itself in front of my eyes

I am a Palestinian war child
This is my story
And this is my only dictionary.

I am Palestine

by Jamie Hamideh

Home to many
muslims and christians
around the world
I live, I have survived
Every day, I endure

I am Historic Palestine
I have a right to live
I have not expelled
but have been expelled
tormented and oppressed,
tortured and tyrannized

I am Palestine
I'm not about power
but I am about freedom
Such when all three
would worship in peace
what a wonderful thing

I am Glorious Palestine
I am brave
I've withstood crimes,
promises and lies
But I will always have faith
May God help me prevail

The Motherland

by M. Jamal Barakat

You can uproot as many trees as you want;
but the roots of my people, my heritage, and my soul
shall forever cultivate my homeland.
Roses of resistance shall sprout from
your concrete oppression
and fruits of pride shall blossom in the midst of
your evil and cold winters.
The beaming rays of justice WILL shine down upon
your shadowed reign;
incinerating your unjust ways
and revealing the truth for all of the world to see.
And my people may return to cultivate their land
with the hands the earth has so dearly yearned for.
And the innocent laughter of children may ring
along the melodies of the rejoicing birds singing
upon the enlivened olive trees.
Hear my words
fear their meaning,
thy oppressive existence shall see its final day,
and exist no more.

Mum Said Free

by Jack Shaka

I admire the flowing river
Serene and free
Going to that place of freedom
Where I am yet to go
Going there – where mum said free

I am going there
To that place of mercy
Where violence and impunity
Murder and Torture exist not
Going there – where mum said free

I am a 13yr old
Orphaned by war
I am the face of the war
That child in the posters
Going there – where mum said free

Fatigue weighs me down
And the hunger drags me down
As I claw on... on...
Holding on... holding on...
Going there – where mum said free

Mama is long gone
Papa too lays gone
And yonder my destiny lies
Mama – where is free?
Going there – where mum said free

Touch my face again Mama
Whisper to me Mama
Protect me from peril
Tell me where free is
Going there – where mum said free

The dust rises Mama
I am engulfed – Can't see
I am besieged by horror
The end is near but where is free?
Going there – where mum said free

Behold my child
Break not anchor
Believe my words
Be brave – shall find free
Go there – where mum said free

While the World

by Afnan Jabr Alqadri

While the world sings a lullaby;
To rock their cribs back and forth;
Strangled hopes cry;
By those living in a dead part of the world!
While the world sings a lullaby;

To rock themselves to sleep;
Desperate dreams fly by;
Are they no longer worth to keep?
While the world is in a coma;

Blinded from head to toe;
Are they truly blinded?
Or are they pretending not to know?
And they rock their cribs;

Back and forth;
Back and forth;
Back and forth;
While a lullaby of certain death;
Is grasping its final breath;
Behind unjust bars!

Requiem

by Jack Shaka

Bombs and bullets strike us
And leave us hurt and bare
Taking all that it can
All that we love and hate
obliterated never to breathe

Requiem after requiem
Today was Ibrahim and Peter
Yesterday was Hannah and Amina
Today again it is Mohamed and John
Tomorrow it shall be you or me

Oh death...
Why strike us and leave us bare?
Why take all that we love?
Oh God...
Why do you permit it?
Oh Allah...
Why don't you stop them?

Right now...
The cold engulfs my being
And the rain begins to drop
But I stand with my brethren
It is another requiem
Another life gone
An innocent!

As the body goes down
A tear drops down my cheek
Then a sob – then a burst
For how long will it go on?
How long shall I cry?
Requiem after requiem
For how long shall I grieve?

Six years old... only six years old
Oh Allah... Oh God...
Why didn't you save her?
Why do you let such a rose
Be taken so soon?
Why do you permit it!

Oh... oh...These children of war
Suffer and die in fights they know not
Oh... oh...
Another requiem – another child gone
A future Imam or even a Rabbi
A president or even an athlete
All never to be
Taken so young.

No longer shall we be caged
Our mouths no longer sealed
Our voices no longer echo
Our priority – saving these innocents
No more requiems please
Let the sun rise with a new hope
A new dawn, a new start.

Zionism

by Khadija Hasan

Israeli missiles into Lebanon,
Hezbollah blamed by Israel again
Hamas defence against occupation
Implicitly sanctioned by United Nations
Expansion in West Bank funded by World Bank
Kids with no shoes throwing stones at the tanks
$30 billion from Obama through tax that you paid
given to Israel in the next decade
Leaving the country is now deemed a crime
crossing the road crosses enemy lines
Penning them in or forcing them out
Human rights law is something to flout
Gaza a death zone kids without homes
Crying for Daddy who will never come home.
Abused turned abuser Zionists claim
That 'holocaust' only refers to their pain.
Recreating scenes from the Nazi Regime
What does extermination of the Palestinians mean?
Now in exile from their homeland
An exodus after a plague on the land?
A familiar story that is told of the Jews
Update the Bible, it's still in the news
Land promised by God to the 12 tribes of Israel?
All Arabs too are descendants of Ismail
Abraham's children born of a slave

Is that a reason to dig them a grave?
NO! Marks and Spencer
NO! Coca Cola
Liberation for Palestine is the New World Order

Palestine

by Ayman Jamal Abdelkarim

I grew up knowing about you,
Heard and read about you,
I sympathized with you,
I cried a tear for you,
I learned to learn for you,
My eyes adored you,
My heart unquestionably loved you,
They said they did and I do,
I swear I would give everything to you,
But I always wonder if you know me,
Who I am and what I came to be,
I'm your son and a son for you I will always be,
The day your sun rises is the day the moon will set on your sea,
O beauty, what have you done to me?
Churches rang their bells, mosques called for prayers... To a
    God we will always seek,
By my words I hope volumes will speak,
For your agony I suffer down beneath,
I bled painlessly in my safe keep,
I dream relentlessly for your peace,
O Palestine, if you only knew what you mean to me...

Oppression No More, Oppression No More

by Brian Joseph Ranum

Oppression no more, Oppression no more
Just put that right foot through the door
Another meaning has been hidden and it's just not a war
It's never ending greed, silence, & apathy
With pleading eyes searching & forgotten peace
Oh my God, why are they looking back at me?
Oppression no more, Oppression no more
For every one that laid down his sword
Another two picked it up & it's just not a war
Scheming ambition misguiding the world
This wasn't the plan meant to unfurl
Oh look, is that a flag held by a little girl?
Oppression no more, Oppression no more
It's a shame that it's all torn
Another hope has been born & it's just not a war
How many times can one weep?
Disturbing lies leading sheep
Why not just set the people free?
Oppression no more, Oppression no more
Leave domination at the door
Another mind has opened & it's just not a war
An intuitive embrace waving an olive branch
No one is higher than another, the tea is in the glass
Will you grant us peace at last?

Reflection

by Jamal Krayem Kanj

After given it much thought
I wonder why life is sought
Living… why ask for more
Unjust world of conquest and war
And I still wonder what life is for
They claim the big fish eats the small
But we humans, eat it all
In a new world order of domination and thrall
I still wonder if life is worth a recall
Humans first fought for grazing rights
Then exploitation reached new heights
Where greed evolution led them to far places
To conquer new land and native races
I still wonder about life's bases
But I have realized of late
That it is not life I must hate
Yet, I still wonder, is life that great?
It is human doublespeak and hypocrisy
It is the false promise of democracy
It is the new world power autocracy
Where killing and vengeance is a self fulfilling prophecy
Humanity need redefine
Self interest and political malign
For the human character is not divine
I now know why life is repine

A Leader to Lead Us to Sing

by Fadi Zanayed

As I watch the clouds outside my window flow
Flow across the sky rather slow
I can only wonder about the pace
The pace of independence without an ace
An ace is a leader who can move
Move a people into a groove
Nelson Mandela led the South Africans
Mahatma Gandhi led the Indians
Martin Luther King led the American Blacks
A leader of such a caliber our struggle lacks
At our Diaspora, we need to reflect
To see why there has been neglect
Why are we the only people not free?
Do we not look around and see
Independence the Moroccans did gain
The Sudanese did the same
Libya won its freedom from Italy
The Algerians fought the French rather mightily
What has happened in the last 60 years?
Surely, there have been many tears
Deir Yasseen lives within my soul
Sabra and Chatilla created a hole
A hole in my heart
Jenin took away any part
Any part left of my conscience
And left me without any patience
In 1964 as the PLO was formed, we were hopeful

In June 1967, those hopes became sorrowful
In the 1970s hijackings gave us a name
The label of terrorists caused us pain
Tel al-Zaatar added more suffering
Our hopes were crumpling
Camp David only offered autonomy
The 1980s provided sobriety
And we recognized the existence of the enemy
That handshake in 1993 lives in infamy
As the Peace Accords were signed on the White House lawn
We believed it was the beginning of a new dawn
Into complacency our minds did then dwell
Thinking the struggle was over and all was well
But as we were drafting and signing
The Israelis were cunning and planning
They gave us limited autonomy over populated parts
Divided us in Zones A, B and C on the charts
Then they controlled our movements within these zones
And all they really gave us was bones
The time to travel between Beir Zeit and Ramallah
Has increased by tenfold, Ya Allah!
The Israelis buy time
Using American taxpayers' dime
The longer a peace agreement they elude
The more settlements become glued
All the while, our homes they demolish
In the press they polish
Polish the truth and hide the atrocities
As they torture our people and our cities
They build a wall as our hands are tied
A wall that President Carter called apartheid

The greatest hope we have known
Were the children of the stone
But they were pre-empted in midstream
As secret negotiations in Stockholm came like a dream
Only to lead to a second Intifada episode
Only time will tell when we will again explode
In South Africa Mandela did write
Something he perceived to be quite right
He said the policies of the Apartheid Government of South
    Africa did impose
An armed struggle as the people fought and rose
Rose up against the oppression
And so must we against the occupation
To make salt Mahatma Gandhi did march to the sea
A non-violent movement he did oversee
A champion of the people was he
Fighting peacefully to set his people free
Non-violence was advocated by Martin Luther King
As a bus boycott to Montgomery Alabama he did bring
He was remindful of the past
As he proclaimed that one day his people will be 'Free at last'
Where is our Mandela, Gandhi or King
Who can lead us out of the clouds and to sing
Biladi, Biladi, Biladi
Lecky Houbi Lee Wa Fouadi

Hey Soldier Man

by Dawn Scott

Hey soldier man look down at me,
Try not to ignore that I'm only three
Remember the park they made you destroy,
I played there many times with my friends and my toys.
You see that school, the one over there,
   I was listening to my teacher when she told me to care.
So I promise not to be mad at you,
   It's your job that makes you do what you do.
Maybe you have children and maybe they are three,
Maybe they look real similar to me.
I hope you never have to do it again,
And I hope maybe someday we can be friends.
Soldier I know you can understand,
What it's like for a kid to live in these lands.
I need a home with shelter and love,
Both parents to raise me and God up above.
You're welcome to visit and your family too,
But why not go home and see how we do.

1948

by L. Al-Ahmad

Blindfolded nightmares
of opened floodgates
and disillusioned fates
drowned in that spring of '48

I am drenched
in regret
as I try to accept
that I am no longer home
that it is *I*
who is unknown
in this world
as I roam
and turn every stone
seeking my identity
that may be
hiding
in Jenin
or lost
in Deir Yassin.

It must only be a dream
but I *fear* what I *feel*
that it is all too real
as my heart hits the bottom
overpowered
by the tides

buried
beneath the lies
and all the whys
and the sighs
weighed down
by the guilt
of leaving your side
in that spring of '48.

The Old Man

by Samiha Abusharkeh

I looked at his thin, aged face
Each line represented a massacre
Each wrinkle, a dead son
Each groove, a year of occupation

The keffiyeh hugged his ancient hair
'It's not gray cause I'm old,
They made it gray.'
His agal wrapped around his head and protected him
At least they couldn't take that away like they did his son
'Martyr or prisoner?'
His hazel eyes already told me, 'Both.'

My blood, my Arab blood, was dying for a story
He poured us coffee in tiny Turkish cups
His little tent was terribly comfortable
The sheepskin carpet was soft
The fake Persian rug roof hid me from the sun
But then again there is no sun in Gaza
Or Jenin, or Ramallah, or Al-Khalil, or Jerusalem
Or, or, or

'Before they came, my land, my fields were beautiful
You could eat an apple, bury its core, and the next day
A field of apple trees would grow
My soil was luscious like my wife's hair. She's dead, too.
Then they came and bulldozed it

They took my youngest son
The only one that was left
He was only fifteen.'

He stood up and took me to a barbed wire fence
Where we could see the remnants of his fields
The glory and grandeur that was Greece and Rome are nothing
Nothing
Nothing to this old man's ravaged ruined land
'Look here, my olive trees used to grow here
Oh, see these? Used to be my almond and date trees
I lost all my teeth but if I could still eat from my land, by God
    I would.'

'They ask me "why didn't you leave when you could?"
If you had a paradise like this, would you leave it?'

We kept walking around the agonizing acres
Holding onto the fence to keep our footing
'When they took him, I told them he was the only one that
    could help me
"You killed all my other sons, leave me this one
I am an old man
Who will help me plow my fields?"
You think I didn't love my son? No. I did.
They don't know what love is, so I had to talk business for
    them to hear
He wrote many letters to me after they took him
I couldn't read them because he was right handed
He only had his left hand.'

'One day, he wrote to me not to plow the fields
"Baba, I hid weapons under the ground."
They soon came and plowed my fields searching
They found nothing
"My son, the guns aren't there, what are you talking about?"
"Now you don't have to plow the fields, Baba."

The Apartheid Israeli Wall

by Fadi Zanayed

Imagine if you will this day
A wall surrounding Any Town, USA
Let's say it is Peoria in the heartland
Occupied and surrounded by an apartheid band
Only one gate allows passage outside
To which the residents must abide
The gate is open only in three intervals
A total of fifty minutes – at this one marvels

But wait and listen to me
For there is more to hear and see
Children rush the gate in the morning
To cross to their school through the opening
If in the afternoon the Apartheid soldier forgets to open the gate
The school children for dinner they will be late
Waiting outside until the night opening
Waiting alone along the crossing

But wait and listen to me
Should you happen to be
Happen to be pregnant and in need
In need of a hospital to deliver your seed
No cars may leave through the gate
This is how they subjugate
As this is a way to enslave
The residents inside the enclave

But wait and listen to me
For there is much more I can tell thee
The agriculture of the town is outside the wall
The intention of the apartheid is to haul
Rather to confiscate the land around
Preventing the owners from tilling the ground
As only the very young and very old can pass through
Can pass through the gate leaving workers with nothing to do

But wait and listen to me
Listen to this I beg and plea
Water wells are confiscated
For residents to be motivated
Motivated to leave in time
Leave the place called the bread basket of Palestine
This is a well laid plan
A well laid plan the Apartheid State of Israel did design

But wait and listen to me
If you have a brother you want to see
The wall sometimes cuts through the middle
Middle of the town and does fiddle
Fiddle with relationships and relatives
As on either side each one lives
The Apartheid occupiers do not care
As they divide, split and flare
Flare the emotions and leave them in despair
A policy to uproot the residence is in the air

But wait and listen to me
This is not Peoria you see
This is Qalqilya in Palestine
The conditions are not fine
The town's people are in a prison
For that Apartheid Israel is the reason
Building a wall that does divide
Dividing people on either side

Sound Bites

by Safiyyah Abdullah a.k.a. Phenomena Da Poet

WE are a people of Reality TV
That is, we are a people of sound bites.
We watch TV and think that someone's week…
that is 168 hours, which is 10,080 minutes,
weed that down to 36 minutes
(after time out for commercials)
is the whole story…
And we watch it fervently,
Diligently,
Determinately,
Slavishly,
No, make that slave-ish-ly…
Because that is what we have become…
Slaves to the sound bites of society.
Never taking the time
to train our minds
to find what is behind
these sound bites.
So let me give you some sound bites of my own:
Sound Bite:
Most populated real estate on the face of the earth: Gaza
Sound Bite:
50% of the population is under 18
Sound bite:
52% of the population lives below poverty.
And that was 36 months ago,
before the economic embargo.

Sound Bite:
This densely populated area is walled off on all sides, preventing
materials, food, supplies, and people from getting in or out.

DAY ONE:
Sound Bite:
Lunchtime shopping
Kids coming home from school
Sister across the street had a miscarriage
because there wasn't enough food to eat...
Funeral yesterday... cousin died of dysentery
No medicine shipments in a month of Sundays
Bread lines 13 hours long,
Sound Bite:
Zainab, mother of 3, boiling water
To soak the peas, make the tea,
and soften the day old bread for her daughter
til her 10 year old son gets home with more...
WHOOSH! BANG!
Sound Bite:
Zainab flies across the room...
sits up in a daze
automatically makes her way
across the kitchen...
Got to turn off the gas...
What was it that caused that blast?
Another follows and wails begin
while mothers pour out in the streets and holler
their children's names...
Searching streets for children who
were just playing games,

or coming from school,
or standing in line waiting for water or fuel
WHOOSH! WHOOSH! BANG! BANG!
Sound Bite:
Here comes more missiles once again
Sirens blaring… then silent
As missiles hit police stations,
fire houses
civilian populations
already under siege
now besieged by F15s
Paid for with US dollars…
Make that our dollars
taken from food stamp programs
And education scholar-
ships firing missiles from the Israeli navy
Hitting families
playing on beaches
just longing for a small distraction
from a long life long of occupation…

DAY TWO:
Sound Bite:
Hospitals overflowing… beds, floors with rivers of blood
    pouring
No way to triage the wounded
Lives, as always, in God's hands.
Doctors slipping on blood soaked
floors as they struggle
to treat bodies burned and mangled.
Hospitals turning away injured.

No room inside or out
as minute by minute the death count
Rises
as the bombing continues another day
and Gaza is deafened by the world's silence
Sound Bite:
Bodies litter the streets.
There's a young girl's hand
still clenching her book,
next to it an old boot
within it the foot
of an elderly man who once ran
trying to save her
as she stood frozen with fear

DAY THREE:
Sound Bite:
More of the same
Israel saying they're only playing a game
Started by Hamas
Alas,
Did we forget?
The ceasefire was violated election day
Nov 4,
When the Israeli Army
invaded the Gaza Strip?
Or did we just miss that sound bit?
Sound Bite:
Israel saying they warn the civilians before
dropping bombs
Give them a call on their telephone:

Ring... Ring... Hello, you there under siege that have nowhere
to go...
This is the Israeli Army just placing a courtesy call telling you
we are about to drop in your neighborhood for a friendly
visit.
Or was that a bomb hit.
Doesn't matter...
ain't got no phone anyway...
and all the lines and satellites have been hit by the second day.

DAY FOUR:
Sound Bite:
Worldwide demonstrations galore
As concerned citizens pour
out into the streets
Begging someone to put an end to this
Genocide and massacre...
But once again just being ignored...

DAY TEN:
Sound Bite:
Ground assault begins
Carnage and destruction no end
Gaza is now a patchwork quilt.
And still there's no guilt
when schools are bombed
and weaponless children are killed and harmed.
Sound Bite:
Ceasefire in place
For supplies and water
While the Israeli Army is ordered

To *continue* its ground assault.
Again only silence – no comments
about this blatant double talk.
So ladies and gentlemen
of privileged conditions,
I apologize for ruining your peace and serenity
with my sound bites of another's reality
but maybe tonight
when you kiss your children
goodnight
these sound bites
will replay in your sleep
and you will become outraged...
decide to become engaged...
decide find the courage
to enter the sound stage
and stop listening to sound bites.

Red Roofs

by Gerald Lenoir

Red roofs, the color of blood, dot the stolen hillsides.
Walls are erected that scar the sacred soil –
Violating ancient vineyards, separating people from familial
  places,
Cutting off communities, culture and commerce.
A whole country, an entire people in Bantustan bondage
Exploited, evicted, expropriated, expelled, exterminated
In the shadow of the Wailing Wall, Al-Aqsa and Via Dolorosa.
In Hebron, Abraham and Sarah turn in their graves.
In Deheisheh, children grow up amid unholy terror.
Apartheid in the Holy Land.

Little Boy, Little Boy

by Zaheera Rahim Warmbaths

The storm between each heartbeat
Laid waste to his soulless feet
Body desecrated beyond recognition
His eyes left without vision

Just two was his age
Little boy, little boy
Seeking refuge in the clouds
His Palestinian heart Unattainable, lost and never to be found

Pieces of his arms, his lungs, his smile
Scattered upon the mirage of fearless ground
Little boy, Little boy

Rivers of blood
Fountains of tears
All rise to the flood
That had been collecting for years
Little boy, little boy

Worry not for your land
What you have witnessed today
No being could ever believe
But rest easy for all shall be well
Up in Janatul-Firdous
Where you all shall forever dwell.

A Slideshow Plays.

by Afnan Jabr Alqadri

A slideshow plays,
since the day of the 27th of December,
I try pausing every image,
working on deleting them
from my memory
but all the images stay
They Stay...
and when the slideshow is done,
It Replays and Replays,
And the world is watching,
sitting with tobaccos in their hands,
In a worm cafe,
While I am battling
Every Single Day!!
A slideshow plays,

since the first day I was alive,
so count the years,
with the images that are still alive,
and think of the days
that I count down
till the day life would be Deprived
And all the images Stay,
They Stay,
and they increase every single day,
and the world is still watching
Like it's okay

they are created from Souls,
and I'm created from Clay!
A slideshow plays,

Since yesterday, tomorrow,
and another thousand years,
and the images Stay,
They Stay,
carrying with them,
billions of tears,
of innocent children,
who live on fears,
and the world will never change;
will never interfere,
and the slideshow
will play Everyday!!

Fly Bird Fly

by Fadi Zanayed

Whistle in the night
Somber moment without light
I welcome the song of the bird For days the only sound I've
heard
The song of freedom chirping in the air
Ironically I am a prisoner of despair
Fly bird fly in support of those who care for you
Go and fight for what we are due
Prosper mentally in our cause
Become a leader who knows when to pause
Build conviction, honor and determination
Build democracy into a nation
Fly bird fly letting your wings stretch across the sky
Encompass within your wings all within our pie
The whole without all its sum is but a part
Be a leader who is brave and smart
Build a consensus while respecting the call
The call to honor and respect for us all
My captors have brought supper for me to eat
Stay and feast before the duty you have to meet
Whistle in the night
Then I'll know your path is right
Remember me as I linger in jail
Rescue me before I grow old and frail
I will be with you night and day
I am your conscience in the words you say
Bless the children who throw the stone

It is in their eyes that we see what we own
Condemn the hypocrisy of those who occupy
They see not the history of why they cry
Be good, self-righteous and fair
People will listen over the air
Neither harm nor be harmed in the course you take
Rather set your mark and plant your stake
For here is the line you must draw
While respecting international law
The world will then see us within our right
Using civil disobedience not our might
Fly bird fly letting your energy soar
Free me to Palestine once more

Palestine

by Mo Mohamed

America's 9/11
Is Palestine 24/7
Rest in peace to all, enjoy heaven

Every life is worth the same as another
Because in the end we all are brothers
A Palestinian body can't be a trophy
When with every Israeli death the world turns on Gaza slowly

All the hatred because of stolen land
When they could be living hand-in-hand
Let the Palestinians go to Dome of the Rock
Without being penetrated by AK shots
Worshipping Allah is their only mission
Not every Muslim is motivated by terrorism

Terrorism comes both ways though
You think you do, but you really don't know
The Geneva Conventions mean nothing to Netanyahu
Israel, look what you make America do

American eyes are blind
They only see what FOX News finds
Israel has never been guilt free
Jerusalem is property of Falisteen

Peace Process

by L. Al-Ahmad

They speak of a **resolution**, but we know it's an illusion
created to conceal the motives
of prolonging this process
of unjust persecutions
of continuing **exile** and **repression**
and the endless **dispossession**
of a land trampled by oppression.

They speak of **tolerance** and even **acceptance**
in the journey of this 'process' that has left us stateless
A process that has lost its objectives,
where peace is subjective to a terrorist's perspective
on what should encompass **justice.**

They speak of **security** and the possibility of flexibility
and the easing of the sieging
but all they're doing is appeasing
the world
using 'peace' as the reason to promote treason
being committed within our nation.

They speak of **developments** but all we see are *settlements*
as they proceed with the **demolitions** and **evictions**
an array of contradictions
not to mention the **restrictions** and unwarranted **convictions**
under the occupier's jurisdiction.

They speak of **humanity** and demand of us **humility**
for granting us the **opportunity** to live with
limited **accessibility**
in their fenced in facility.

Yet we maintain our dignity in hopes for an opportunity
to regain our **mobility** and bypass their **incivility.**
So that we may harness additional strength,
and have the courage to stand against
a process which seems to have no ends
since *peace is not what this 'process' intends.*

Could it be her?

by Fadi Zanayed

Over there next to that child
That elderly woman with the embroidered dress
It looks like the one Grandma always wore
The traditional dress which represents our hometown
The detail, the patterns, the style are distinctive to each town
Could it be her?
Look at those eyes they look like Grandma's eyes
They are hazel brown eyes rich with color
There is happiness and sadness within those eyes
For deep within them are our memories
The Nakba, the Six-Day War, our family history
Could it be her?
Her face looks so much like Grandma's face
There is smoothing warmth in her look
The complexion, the lines, the wrinkles, each tell a story
Like the rings of a tree they have a history
Her wedding day, my father's birth, death of Grandpa
Could it be her?
Her hands look like Grandma's hands
Look at her hands all aged, spotted and dark
Those are the hands of a worker in the fields
Those are the arms that comforted me
The hugs, the kisses while in those arms
Could it be her?
Her voice is much like Grandma's voice
It's soft and soothing yet commanding
I slept listening to her voice tell me folk tales

From her words I learned who I am
Our traditions, our culture, our existence as a people
Could it be her?
It could not be for my Grandma has long past on
Her dress still lives in our clothing
Her eyes still give us vision
Her face still gives us hope
Her arms still gives us strength
Could it be her?
It is her within us all
We are her through our traditions
We are her through our folk tales
We are her through our weddings
We are her, we are her, we are her
A Journey to See Where I Was To Be

Borders of the Heart

by Asma Haidara

The lobbyist demagogue
Preaching from synagogue
Commands us to kneel with shame at the border
Because he wants all of God's land
Hoarder
He shouts, spiteful with pride
Forgetting the tears his ancestors cried
As I am driven out like they once were
Like our old Bedouin Mother
Sent to roam deserts with despair
With Ishmael
But God quenched them
With the waters of paradise
And raised them up
And made them a great nation
Rise again,
Oh you Children of Ishmael, you are a great nation.

Colourless Days

by L. Al-Ahmad

I sought out to define my days to my captor.
He stared on at a loss as the walls listened to my tale.
And here, I begin.

The days are a journey
an endless climb
to the heights of the bottoms.
The days bring on a mist of woe
from the lost tryst of those
lovers.
The days twist tales
and convey a masochist's elations
from his warped imagination.
The days end when the start begins
and begin as burdens
on my children
also held within this prison.

He stared on un-amused
by the lack of colour in my explanation
but I continued on regardless
since all the colours left in frustration.
The days have washed away
the rosy cheeks of my children.
Their blushing flirts
once danced bare
are paled by despair

and what is left is found
in the depth of the eyes
that bore witness
to the theft of the days.
And it is there
that the burdens of black and grey
attempt to outweigh
their untainted hearts of white.

The days are filled with lines.
Lines to wait.
Mark an x by your name.
Outlines and parameters.
Bars and stripes.
Lines to check – checkpoint.
Lines that trace the anguish
upon the face of the oppressed.
Lines that snake the borders of my prison;
and lines within those lines that keep me away from my worship.
Lines that black out the identity on the deed to my land,
putting a light out on my *right to return*.
Lines on my palms cut short by your doing.
Lines on my paper that are filled with rhymes and truths.
Green lines and armistice lines
Boundary lines and creeping lines which encroach on my days.
Lines which encroach on my days…
Inching deeper into my dreams of tomorrow.

The walls understood
and apologized for standing still
while helping him keep me in

trapping me in my own mind
without my freewill
Surrounding me in my history
in the agony of stolen memories
of what used to be all of me.

My Favorite Color Was Red!

by Afnan Jabr Alqadri

Woke every morning;
Looking for my favorite T-shirt;
Got furious if I didn't find it;
Got mad if my mom hid it;
She told me that I grew older;
That my T-shirt won't fit;
But I was four years old;
My shirt to me was gold;
Grieving over a shirt;
Till I fell asleep in bed;
All because that T-shirt was red!

How innocent was I!
A piece of red cloth used to make me cry;
Never thought a color that used to attract me as a kid;
Would make me wish all colors would be forbid;
Never thought a color I used to adore;
Would one day be lying on my bedroom floor;
That red color that was once dear to my heart;
Did so much to my childish heart.

People all around just stood and stared;
I knew all of them were aware;
I was still only a child;
I did nothing wrong;
I just stood there;

Waiting for a reasonable respond;
to WHY!!

The 27th of December 2008;
I remember that day crystal clear;
I was never a bright child;
But I learned the numbers from fear;
counting days wishing the end would be near;
counting 1..2..3 skipping 4 and 5 and jumping to 6;
was how I usually count numbers;
I remember my brother collecting sticks;
Then asking me to prepare a red color mix;
To color the sticks to teach me how to count right;
But the red mix dried up;
And blood covered the sticks instead;
covered it up with the color red;
And from that day till now;
I can't believe my brother is dead!

I saw one of our neighbors who lived next door;
Carrying him straight to my room;
Screaming and yelling in a way I never heard before;
And I saw my brother's red blood on every spot on the floor;
I even remember the smell;
It was the smell of goodbye, I could tell;
I remember seeing one of his sticks lying in my room;
I picked it up and went near my bro;
Held his hand in a way I would never let go;
Just watching tears overflow;
Over a fellow who meant a lot to me;
And the Whole World should know!

One of my relatives came up to me;
Placed his hands on my eyes;
Expecting me to believe nothing's wrong;
Through all those tears and cries;
Expecting me to forget the scene I saw;
Wondering if this is an unwritten law;
To kill an innocent child!

Wrapping him with a white shroud;
As if he was a new born child;
His face was bright;
His eyes closed tight;
And his face lit up with a smile;
His smile really irritated me;
Thinking if he could smile then he could see;
Everyone wanting him back;
But he was gone;
And I will never move on!

All went to the yard;
To burry my innocent bro;
I was in shock, I decided not to go;
I was left in my room staring at a red colored floor;
Recalling the memories of a color I used to adore;
Tearing my blanket, and my tiny shirt I found;
'The shirt my mom hid', I said to myself
Then I started weeping with no sound;
I tore my shirt to pieces to release my heart's pain;
Then I said with a calm voice;
I Hate You Red You Are To Blame!!

Confession

by L. Al-Ahmad

Did you love her? – I did.

Did you defend her? – I will.

Did you help her? – I am trying.

Did you weep for her? Endlessly.

Do you understand her? We share one soul.

Will you denounce her for your freedom? She is my freedom. Her pain is my sorrow. Her name is my purpose. Her place exists.

Convict me! For I am suffering.

Convict me! For I am not me if she is not free.

Convict me and jail me in her arms.

Beaten by your lies. Kicked by your hypocrisy. Starved from justice. Robbed of her children. She remains.

So convict me for loving her. Convict me for honoring her. Convict me and let us mourn together for she has been damned to your prisons. Convict me and I will lay by her side until she regains her strength.

Together, we will break the shackles at her feet and follow the roots of her fruits until we find the light behind the veil of your occupation.

Cruel Dream – Cruel Reality

by Maher Massis

My beloved country
it has been over forty years
since I have last seen you

Do you look the same
do you miss me
do you miss me

I have often dreamt about you
I dreamt that I was a child
sleeping beneath a fig tree
dreaming about what I will be
a shepherd, a farmer, a teacher
in my land, in my land

But then in my dream
I heard a sudden rumble of the Earth below
an earthquake I thought
no – it can not be

Should I flea from the trees
or stand firm and save the trees
being uprooted from the monster below
the monster I have yet to know

I waited for the rumbling to end
but to no avail
and then suddenly in my dream
the rumbles turned into liquid earth
blasting from the redness below
smoking the skies above
choking the air to breath

Should I flea
should I flea I thought
no, my instinct told me
no, for I must see
the monster yet to be

I waited and waited
to the point of exaltation
then finally the monster arose
from the hell below

It was an ugly thing
that was all green
with spears of fire

It was human-like
but I could not see
but only one mark
on its metal head
the star of David
the star of David

I cried out
'leave my land!
leave my land!'
but the monster kept coming
closer and closer to me

I stood my ground
and grasped an olive branch
naively waving it
to warn the people
to warn the people

but the monster responded
by burning all the trees
to the ground

Then the monster grabbed me
and I struggled and struggled
then all of a sudden
I had awoken from my dream
as a soldier of Israel
was banging my head
against an olive tree
'what are you doing here
go away – go away he ordered!'

How strangely I thought
for I have become the monster
in reality
while in my dream
the true monster resides

Obama: America is Same

by Jamal Krayem Kanj

When you became the leader of the strongest nation
America gained global respect and admiration
Your election was America's final salvation
I thought, America has finally seen the light
At last, it elected someone bright
I thought hate was transformed
And America's politics were finally reformed
But now, it's all the same
America has gained back its shame
The change you promised was in color
None has evolved, not even the shade of US dollar
The change was only from a dull white
To a lively black might
The hopefuls were let down
The poor, black, white and brown
The hope you bode
Turned the smile into frown
The change you vowed
Disappeared like a steam
In a late night dream
And Congress is back to its old theme
Docile to Israel's blackwhite autocracy
A nation ruled by a Jewish theocracy
But in name, it's a democracy
The mother of all political hypocrisy

Under you Obama, America is the same
It has gained back its shame
For your promise of change is lame

Gaza at Night

by Jackson Moulding

The sky monsters as black as night
Come prowling looking for a fight.
Cradled close I can smell her
The scent of mum it soothes me over.

There's nothing else that we can do
But lie in wait till morning's due.
The beating of my mother's heart
The sound of buildings ripped apart.

The whistling before the big bright flash
Holding hands we make a dash.
Lifted, twisted, we are flying
The bed is spinning where we were lying.

My ears are burning with the roar
The boom I've never heard before.
Floating, a moment, time holds on
And then everything is gone.

The ground erupts and swallows me
Or is it the ceiling? I can't see.
Which way is up? I knew before
It's dark and cold, and I am raw.

My hand mummy, we're holding tight
Everything is going to be alright.
Don't let me go, I need you more
You know that I am nearly four.

Dark and fire, rubble and mud
Or is it earth mixed up with blood?
I move my body, but not much,
My chin and cheek I cannot touch.

I call my mum, as my face is sore
Up cuddle me from the floor.
We never let go, our fingers entwined
A greater love you'll never find.

I need her now, I need her grace
I want her to touch my face.
I pull her hand from the floor
I have her hand and nothing more.

1948

by J.M. Zahria

A land with people they claim was vacant
My grandfather, a figure of imagination
His house invisible
His olive trees mythical
They settled on our lands stolen from our hands
They burned our rights away
They blundered our world in 1948

The world cries falsely in their favor
Their Media lies remain unwavered
The 'terrorists' that exist in Gaza
are no different from those in Warsaw
Genocide under Nazi abuse
No one denies what you went through

Victims transform into sullen oppressors
Caution; you're protected by a fallen empire
You have the power to make peace
Yet you demean and mislead
We are victims of oppression
Stop denying your aggression
The abuse, the torture, the brutal occupation
You are to blame for our total subjugation

You divide and conquer us extremely well
The cracks of your superiority are starting to swell
Change will come despite your disapproval
A new Middle Eastern bright revival

The chosen people of God must redeem their sins
Stop using their history to kill Palestinians
No one is perfect we all pray for peace
But you're pointing your gun straight at me
The humiliation and checkpoints conscious by all
The separation barrier, our own wailing wall
Our lands dwindle right before our eyes
The settlements increase as the peace process dies
Negotiations, Peace Talks, Resolutions,
a gimmick of apartheid and further illusion
Time to expand the revolution
Sit down and listen to my solution:

O Palestine,
Freedom comes at a heavy price
Take charge and think twice
Stand up in the face of catastrophe
Success can deliver by our unity
Lead your own momentous destiny
Rid yourselves of your dreadful enmity
Keep your hearts inclined together
Occupied minds wrestle in common
The bond of God no man can separate
The rope of faith no man can break it

1948 an unforgivable tragedy
Crimes of the Nazis followed by treachery
The struggle of our cause
we shall intensify
Their own example shows us
the pain will subside

My Friend from Auschwitz

by Maher Massis

I love you my friend
not for your human flesh
victimized by mortal evil
but for the purity of your soul
farewell my friend, farewell

Behold oh fellow man
remember my friend
remember the ashes
from his naked bones

Hovering above the Earth
as a permanent testament
to the triumph of hell
over man
remember

And yes my friend
the highest pedestal of heaven
will await you
for by virtue of your pedestal
you shall become the overseer
of the committee of forgiveness

It is you that advises the angels of God
to whom should forgiveness be given
to whom should sins be cleared

to whom should eternity be guaranteed

And yes my friend
your brothers and sisters below
depend on you in heaven
to lobby for the forgiveness
of their continuous sins

But I say to you
no man, no soul
nor the great ancient prophets
can forgive future sins
because of past suffering

For it is not your burden my friend
nor is it mine
but only those who seek heaven
by living as pure spirits
dressed in human cloth

Did I tell you my friend
of my nightly dream
a dream about a dream
about my land, my home
about the sweet smell of olives
caressing the temple of my soul
whispering into my ears the songs of Awda
the songs of Return

And when you get lonely my friend
go and visit my brothers and sisters
who were uprooted from the seeds of life
wandering the earthly purgatory
awaiting for the ship of Awda

Many of these souls
have accompanied you to heaven
for the same reason
for the same reason

What do you tell them my friend
when you greet them with empty hands
'Welcome suffering souls of Palestine
for you have left the purgatory earth
in my name
by my brothers and sisters
the house of Israel'

How painful indeed
it is to feel
the pain of your brethren
and thus know that I have become
a victim of those I weep for

Indeed my friend
we need to pray
even in heaven
more than on Earth
for our brethren below

To replace hatred with love
to replace torment with peace
and vengeance with forgiveness

Only then
can my dream and your dream
be sewn together with golden thread
to make a new cloth for man
pure and true

Shooting Stars

by Ben x Jenin

As the Monks marched and fell in Burma,
and freedom seemed to elude another generation,
As the streets flowed red and saffron in Rangoon
Soldiers shooting, slicing, cutting
We were buying, selling, drinking, fucking

As a Palestinian boy hungrily wandered into the Brigades,
raised on loss, denial, want and dead friends
$500 homes exploded by million dollar bombs
Space age weaponry used on refugees
without an earthen jug of water.
Room in your old village for thousands of white Russians
but not for you.
No return, no escape.
I cursed at my television
and went to work
Teaching the ABCs to businessmen's children in Guess Jeans
In a place of neon and punctual buses
Food aplenty and booze too often....
I'm still hungry and running late.
Hungrier than I ever felt in a Palestinian Camp,
Running late, sometimes on full,
Sometimes on empty
In the absence of the sacred

Monks, Mothers, refugees, survivors, campesinos
Inspiration and lighthouses of the realness,
Unwitting architects of my better self
India, Indo, Khmer, Hondurenos, Rangoon
Palestine, habibi, proud as a lion
Keep marching and I will too
Thru the neon haze, back into the view
Of your $500 home
As the doves fly overhead
Late at night
With your kids on our laps
Drinking tea as the lights of Nazareth flicker in the distance
25 or 25,000 miles away
Depending on your passport

Tomorrow night the sky will fall,
Thousands of shootings stars
Reminding us how small we are
How connected we are
in our vulnerability
and common insignificance
Except to each other
and our dreams.

Tomorrow night, in the meteor shower
I'll picture your faces and send you my heart
Stars burn bright until they fall
So too, must we all
Keep shinin that lighthouse thru the black
Cause all I wanna do is find my way back
I will burn brighter for you....

Oh Palestine, O Mother of Mine

by Naida Dukovic

O Palestine, O Mother of Mine
Do you know, you're always on my mind?
I've come to ask, Why are you crying all the time?

I remember you a long time before,
Why aren't you happy anymore?

Melodies played throughout the street
Everyone around had enough to eat

Children were playing safely outside
Laughing, swinging and running to hide

Men sat out drinking their strong, black coffee
While women were out finishing laundry

So much peace and happiness was in the air
Now I don't see it anywhere...

She said, come here and you will see,
They're trying to take Gaza away from me
And now it's under all this, Occupancy

I turned to ask – How could that be!?
Yes, she said, it had been done very methodically

It happened a little at a time
And now they're claiming, she's no longer mine

You see, there were these people that came a time before
And I greeted them here, at the door

You could see they had no home of their own,
And to me, they seemed helpless and all alone

It's my nature to greet guests with hospitality
But I never imagined, they'd step all over me

We said 'Salaam'
They said, 'Shalom'

Had I only known they meant, 'Shell Home'

And yes, that is exactly what they did
Since then, my people have only ran and hid

You know I didn't realize they had a plan,
To come here and take everything they can

Why such anger and so much hate?
It is something my heart cannot tolerate

Such arrogance and utter hypocrisy
There's no such thing here as democracy

O my dear, there was a time
That the kids would be out and played just fine

And now if you look outside the door
You cannot see that anymore
Do you see what they have done?
They have brought their big bad gun

They have put checkpoints at every door
And no one can pass freely anymore

They've taken my men, who grew up so fine
And they have killed them, one at a time

I have raised doctors, engineers, and even more
But they cannot find a job – not one anymore!

My dear people are jailed all the time
Without committing one single crime

My lovely daughters, with eyes so bright,
No longer feel, nor see the light

They've destroyed their homes, schools,
Even from their homes, they've been forced to flee

Can you believe they've been made into a refugee!?
Throughout the years they've shed so much blood
Easily, my son, it could have started a flood

Defending their land with such heroism,
How dare they turn around and call it terrorism!

My tears have been running for years and years
But the world has chosen to cover their ears

But I will tell you this, something they cannot foresee
It is God, and He is here with me
And injustice is not what he wanted for me

God has a plan and one that cannot unfold –
And it is a story that is left untold

He has blessed this land, this beautiful land of mine
And has told me to be patient and I'll be just fine

O Palestine, O Mother of mine
I will tell you this one more time
I will speak out… I will fight… I may even die,
But I will never let them call you, 'Mine'

This is a promise that I make to you
And it is a promise we hold very true
For in our hearts, it's all about you

All this bloodshed spilled everywhere
We all know it's all stemming right from there

We will heal this land and dry your tears
And we will remove from you all your fears

There will be peace someday, God-willing, soon sometime
Because of course we were promised, by the One, Sublime.

Be patient and persevere
Because we know, the end is near

I love you Palestine, O Mother of Mine
Please be strong – It's just a matter of Time.

From a Palestinian Child to God

by Jamal Krayem Kanj

Oh God… please protect my life
For human wickedness is rife
I am too young to die
Phosphorus raining from the sky
Causing my flesh and skin to fry
Then an Israeli lie or a sly
And another news spin
Oh my God where did I sin?
In a large Gaza pen
Exposed heart and skin
There is no place to run
From bombs, rain or sun
Young, old, sisters and brothers

Fathers, babies and mothers
We want to live like all others
But it was in a clear December day
Children having fun and play
When death came with no delay
Concealed in an Israeli phosphorus spray
In all colors and rays
Turning the blue sky into gray
I hide in my mother's arm
To shield me from Israeli harm
Overtaking by fear
Yet, her timid smile heals my tear
To live another day, another month, another year

Oh Israel! I promise to be your nightmare
For the story of my torment I'll share
And victory will bloom out of my despair!

Oppressed I was Born

by Yasir Tineh

Oppressed I was born
Through the stress I evolved
Till I tested the ropes
Blessed with a cause
That possesses me to roar
Obsessed so I express
The mess that press
On my thoughts
Till I free all the globe
Roaming broken roads
Surrounded by corruption
Greed and the depths of the war.

She Said…

by Yasir Tineh

She said don't fear for the end is near
She said don't fear for the end is near
Even if it seems like you've aged but you're still young my dear
Don't fear the end is near
You suffered too much to give up, it's clear
She said don't worry; Love always conquers Evil and so he smiled
Even as his body ached from the pain of oppression
Her words like a song stuck in his mind
Don't fear my dear for the end is near
She tattooed the word freedom on her stitched lips
Her screams unheard by many but to him they're clear
He said don't fear for the end is near
So she smiled as he held her close
She suffered too much to give up, it's clear
He said don't fear, your scars will heal
We're apart but shine like one, on an endless chase
Like the moon and the sun; then the stars spoke and said
Don't fear for the end is near.

Rachel Corrie

by William A. Cook

The picture told the story:
this wisp of a girl defiant
against the armored clad Goliath
Towering above her,
An illustration from the Book of Kings.
This orange-coated giant
Went out from Israel,
The land of the Philistines,
To slaughter the Palestinians.
And he stood six cubits and a span
Above those clustered about their homes.
And he had treaded greaves about the knees,
Sheets of steel about his shoulders,
And shafts thrust forward
To hold his spear, the blade of death.
All who saw him fled in terror
Save this gentle girl,
Who held God's voice in her megaphone.
Did she see the tight curl of his lip
As he sat in his judgment seat
And she stood in the shadow of death?
Did he, when his day was done,
Hose the blood from his blade?
Did he lean against his protective armor
And gaze at the setting sun?
Did he go home that night
And place his yarmulke beside the door?

Did he greet his wife with a loving kiss,
And grasp his daughter tightly to his breast?
And did she, in fear, plead 'Be gentle, dear'?

HESPERUS PRESS

Under our three imprints, Hesperus Press publishes over 300 books by many of the greatest figures in worldwide literary history, as well as contemporary and debut authors well worth discovering.

Hesperus Classics handpicks the best of worldwide and translated literature, introducing forgotten and neglected books to new generations.

Hesperus Nova showcases quality contemporary fiction and non-fiction designed to entertain and inspire.

Hesperus Minor rediscovers well-loved children's books from the past – these are books which will bring back fond memories for adults, which they will want to share with their children and loved ones.

To find out more visit **www.hesperuspress.com**

@HesperusPress